Under A Hundred

A Competition to Honor
Edward Davin Vickers

Georgia Poetry Society

2011

Contents

Forward

This collection is the culmination of many years of effort to honor one of the founders of the Georgia Poetry Society, Edward Davin Vickers.

Vickers, with Charles Bruehler and several inaugural members, founded what was originally called the Georgia State Poetry Society in 1979. Incorporated in 1981 as a 501(c)3 organization, the Georgia Poetry Society today has grown to some 200 members, many of them a prominent and active part of the Georgia poetry "scene."

Ed Vickers unfortunately did not live to see his fledgling venture flourish. Born January 10, 1945 in Grady County, Georgia, he passed away after an extended illness in Fulton County, Georgia on April 17, 1990.

At the time of his passing a memorial fund was established. Those funds remained unused until they were rediscovered in 2008, owing largely to uncertainty about how best to memorialize him. A committee charged with the decision suggested a memorial chapbook series of which this volume is the inaugural issue. We hope you find much pleasure in reading it.

Steven Shields
Editor

Where A Poem Comes From

Ron Self

Still Life with Poet

About some things, Auden said,
they were never wrong, the old Masters;
which is not to say they were infallible; which,
being human, they most decidedly were not.
Thus they could spend weeks, months even,
discovering a masterpiece on canvas or board,
a painting of inanimate objects: still life
with dead pheasants, haunch of venison,
apples, pears, pomegranates; while
elsewhere in the house, wife, children,
mistress are in tatters, bills pile up,
duties, chores are left undone; while
elsewhere in the world, dreadful martyrdoms
run their course, Icarus falls from the sky
to the sea, dogs go about their doggy lives.

Poets on the other hand, are often wrong,
rarely right, revel in our own fallibility,
the uncertainty of almost everything,
particularly words on paper.
We plait our own crown of thorns,
rose, mock orange, a few laurel leaves
woven in for good measure,
place it on our heads, press down,
draw blood that drips into drafts
of poems on the page. And we, too,
spend weeks, months, lifetimes even,
peering through curtained windows,
from the back pew, garden path,
end of the grocery checkout line,
on our backs looking up at clouds,
observing perpetually.

And sometimes, not often, it is as though
the whole world must have known we were coming,
must have known a poet would be looking,
would some day look back, recollect in tranquility
the emotion of this particular moment,
and thus stopped to rearrange, compose
itself into a picture: landscape of rocks,
river, flora and fauna, composition
of quince, cabbage, melon and cucumber
to catch the poet's eye, engage the poet's brain,
summon the poet's muse to come, run the risk,
wade out into the river, scoop up a handful
of quicksilver words, hold them as they spill
through fingers onto the page, into a fruit bowl
of light, shadow, dead birds, squirrel, side of beef:
a still life, a still life with poet in the background.

Written Itself

Having embedded two words side by side
on the same page, the poet sits back to watch and wait,
hoping mutual admiration, concupiscence, will come along,
compel them to touch, stroke, kiss, make love, reproduce
into a family, a family tree arching upward from trunk,
spreading outward to branch to limbs, to multitude of leaves
glimmering, shimmering in the sun, amorous, recumbent
on the white sheet, covered now with words,
with whole generations of words, a poem
that has almost, but not quite, engendered,
almost, but not quite, written itself.

Where A Poem Comes From

The smell of barbecue drifts from somewhere
across the backyard, through the screen porch,
in the open door to the den where the poet sits
trying to write a poem about love and death,
and, suddenly, on the page, an arresting image,
unconscious association of sizzling flesh,
hot fire of passion and the grill, love
as sauce and pickle, Cole slaw, sliced
white bread; death as Boston butt, diced,
chipped, served up in a poem about love,
death and barbecue, a meditation
on where a poem comes from.

Co-authors

Unbeknownst to the poet carrying his plastic
bag of trash out to the curb for collection,
his most fervent reader, most avid fan,
and the greatest living scholar on the subject
of his collected works, published and unpublished,
is the trash man, who, on Tuesdays and Fridays,
stops in front of the poet's house and,
rather than tossing the poet's bag of trash
into the compactor, reverently places it inside
the truck for later excavation and examination,
culling from its contents the garbage-stained
crumpled-up pages of poems in progress,
first drafts, revisions, revisions of revisions,
final version yet to be edited, then edited
through more drafts, revisions and revisions of revisions;
and the trash man saves them all, lines them up
in proper chronological order so he can see
the act of creation from concept to completion
and all the steps in between, which explains why,
on those rare occasions when the poet makes contact
with the trash man, one dropping trash off
as the other picks it up, the trash man will
sometimes say a word, use a turn of phrase,
something vaguely familiar, suggestive,
that causes the poet, back at his desk
a few minutes later, to change a word or two,
revise yet again a poem he and, unbeknownst to him,
the trash man, are working on, writing together.

Ron Self is a lawyer-musician in Columbus and teaches part-time in the College of Business at Columbus State University. He is a past president of the Georgia Poetry Society, and hosts monthly open mic poetry events at libraries in Georgia and Alabama. His poetry has appeared in *Atlanta Review*, *The English Journal*, *Cortland Review*, *Legal Studies Forum*, *Encore*, *Playgrounds Magazine* and various local and state anthologies including *Reach of Song*. He was the 2008 recipient of the Plains Poet Award and the 2010 San Antonio Poets Prize of the National Federation of State Poetry Societies. He is a co-founder and editor of the Brick Road Poetry Press.

Divided By Zero

Francis Alix

Bruised

It started early, before he knew
the alphabet or counted stars.

He bent over his bed,
broken blade of grass,

for a whipping with a leather belt
long as his height,

buckle the size of his father's fist,
for running in the house, spilling milk.

Cracks flamed, father's shouts stung,
yielded his face to salt and water,

flesh to blue-black bruises he wore
like playground dirt on his jeans.

the slightest brush of his pants
scratched, throbbed fresh welts,

pressure from school chairs shot
spikes through legs, spine.

Before gym class, he watched his friends
strip, pull t-shirts, shorts out of bags,

his furrowed brow exploding to wide eyes,
mouth at their undamaged skins.

Perfect Meadow

Holsteins chew in unison,
long stems of blossomed
buttercups sway,
sun stretches fence shadows
at the end of my street.

My childhood is defined
by the wild plain, riding my bike
to Grandma's, mooing
at lowered heads, laughing
at tails fanning overheated flies.

The creatures utter silence,
so focused on their duty
as dairy cows to satisfy
my cravings for chocolate milk,
ice-cream on sugar cones.

I love their spotted skins,
twitching ears, black coat button eyes
tuned to browning grass,
petals curling, falling,
cool breeze tingling wet noses.

I never said goodbye
so suddenly they disappeared,
my mouth soundless at the red,
white, blue For Sale sign among
timbered frames of condos three high.

The crowded street has no room
for my wheels, place for my eyes
to wander but up to the blue landscape
free of screaming brakes, air guns,
open and serene, for now.

Death Wishes of a Young Man

If I die in my eighties,
I don't want to lie in a nursing home,
sheet crease sharp at my throat,
voice vacant as family at my side,
nurses vigilant for closed eyes, unheaving chest.

If I die in my sixties,
I don't want to sit in my cubicle,
fingertips not feeling the clicking computer keys,
air unsure it can enter my lungs,
heart eager to reject its mission.

If I die in my forties,
I don't want to bleed on a sidewalk,
back pocket clawed by a desperate hand,
wallet blooming a smile on the mugger's face,
knife, anger, slammed into my gut.

If I die in my twenties,
I don't want to collapse on a battlefield,
desert sand or grassy plains a makeshift bed,
sun, snow, clothes I can't shed,
surrender welcome as the bullet through my skull.

Francis Alix's poetry chapbook, *Balancing on Unstable Ground*, was published by Červená Barva Press in 2009. His work has been published in many journals, most recently in *Hawai'i Pacific Review*, *Mad Poets Review*, and *Main Street Rag*. His work has won many prizes, most recently from the North Shore Poets Forum in Massachusetts and the Philadelphia Writers' Conference. He is also a playwright, with plays produced in Massachusetts and New York. He is a book and journal reviewer for the *Small Press Review/Small Magazine Review*. He lives in Boston, Massachusetts.

Parsing

Dances for when the music stops

Mildred White Greear

Dreams are real as long as they last. Can we say more
of Life?

—Havelock Ellis, *The Dance of Life*

Dancer

My mother was sober; her joys were controlled.
Something had taught her to hide much of her soul;
only those she locked with her
knew the part that stayed free.

I saw her as dancer, nimble in raindrops,
dancing to music my father's fiddle
could never play.
So delicately dancing
until the sweet dream stopped one day.

My mother's first daughter leapt among stars,
My mother's three sons strode a strong wind,
larger than life, their deeds heroic to see;
far beyond me,

Their worshipful critic,
recorder of their special graces.
Watching each with exquisite awe
I might have been crippled by wonders I saw,

But my loving mother
wisely left me her door,
behind which my words and I
practice our hesitant dance.

Benches

Our benches will not sing for us until our friends have sat upon them.
—from the Finnish epic "The Kalevala"

Dear Friend, you have sat upon our benches;
the whole house sings, beyond the sadness of your leaving.
So everywhere the music, dancing began; all things
have to be restrained. The dining chair
dances so that wine spills and rolls on plastic
cover so judiciously placed over the cotton sheet
masquerading as linen last night for the banquet
where smallest words like fading fireworks landed
and kept clinging to cups, saucers and the crumb cake.
I shake jewel sentences from the careful napkins.

Meanwhile window panes loosen in their frames; I fear
they may shatter from the light of your left-over gaze.
Should this happen, I shall send you great bills from the
    glazier.
He will ask how on earth such a thing occurred
and I will have to confess that we had a sorcerer here.

Do not let the account disturb you. It has, as always
been paid in advance, your company being beyond price,
beyond calculation, even though the house may unsettle
from its foundation. The benches being so out of control.

South Beach, Ossabaw Island, Georgia

My beloveds I have written your names,
giving them to sea and sky
as large as this stick and I can sculpt them
from low tide up to the high berm,
embryo sand castings, letters
gouging ghost shrimp burrows deeply, unevenly.

I disregarded coral skeins, cats' eyes,
fortunes in sand dollars to make
a mile-long reading lesson for gulls;
trenches for crab battles,
deceptive cul-de-sacs in ornamented upper case.

In the long view this writing is permanent
memorial as any; no more fragile connection
with your respective memories or dreams
than stone, whose parent sands I engraved here.

The short meantime is for wonder.
Will subtle re-arrangements of sand strata
forever declare your names backward,
upside down to the earth's center?

Will turtle or tern erase them
With crusty plate or feather before the moon
traces them through dune shadow
for the night birds to read?

My writings here almost violent,
investing a lifetime of energies
directed at loving you, I pray now
that whatever takes them will be quiet.

A froth of what is hardly air, hardly water
whose bonds as they grip the shallowing troughs
deplete further and further…finally implode.
Braille reading your names.

Gone Dancing

Hey, watch out when I dance! When I dance from the inside
It will be like an earth-on-axis whirling;
Everything centered, spinning like mad.

At first I may look like a kite when my arms blur and
disappear
Out there…dancing through fingers, tight skin everywhere.

Up, up on toes, I will be taller than ever I have been!
Everything gone north and south.

I'm telling you, it will be good to reach that high
After all that touching so low.

You may look out and say: *There's a whirlwind out yonder!*
When already it was likely me, blowing your hat off
As I danced right by you. *Right by you!*

And that's no whirlwind out yonder, Kiddos, that's me.
Your mama. Gone dancing.

Parsing

"Gold is where you find it," they have always said.
Such certainty begs other premises
Parsed from life's existential grammar.

Music will be when you hear it.
How you feel it is church.
Love is the always and only because.

Anywhich newborn baby soever at all
Is the who of hope.

Life is while,
And what is to do is to dance
To home, offered as predicate nominative
For gold where you found it to go back to.

Mildred White Greear is a native of Laurel, MS, and recently celebrated her ninety-first birthday. She was for many years an essayist for the *Gainesville Daily Times* and other newspapers. She also taught school in a number of locales as she moved with her family during the WWII years. She spent almost two years in Japan, living in a small village near the airbase where her husband was located.

This work is dedicated to Annell McGee (December 30, 1940 – October 29, 2010).

Acknowledgements

Ron Self: Where A Poem Comes From

"Co-Authors"

Atlanta Review
Legal Studies Forum

Mildred White Greear: Parsing

"Benches"

Chattahoochee Review

"South Beach, Ossabaw
Island, Georgia"

The Old Red Kimono

"Gone Dancing"

At the Edge

www.ingramcontent.com/pod-product-compliance
Lightning Source LLC
Chambersburg PA
CBHW071355130626
46556CB00005B/2198